Before & After
KITCHEN
MAKEOVERS

By Christine E. Barnes

Oxmoor
House®

ISBN: 0-8487-3132-8
Printed in the United States of America
First Printing 2006

Southern Living At HOME®
Senior Vice President and Executive Director: Dianne Mooney
Director of Brand Management: Gary Wright
Research Manager: Jon Williams

Oxmoor House, Inc.
Editor in Chief: Nancy Fitzpatrick Wyatt
Executive Editor: Susan Carlisle Payne
Copy Chief: Allison Long Lowery
Editor: Rebecca Brennan
Senior Designer: Emily Albright Parrish
Copy Editor: Diane Rose
Editorial Assistant: Brigette Gaucher
Editorial Intern: Ashley Wells
Director of Production: Laura Lockhart
Senior Production Manager: Greg Amason
Production Manager: Amorice Nall
Production Assistant: Faye Porter Bonner
Publishing Systems Administrator: Rick Tucker

Before & After Kitchen Makeovers
Managing Editor: Sally W. Smith
Design and Art Direction: Vasken Guiragossian, Amy Gonzalez
Copy Editor/Indexer: Pamela Evans
Principal Photographer: Margot Hartford
Photo Director/Stylist: Cynthia Del Fava
Assistant Stylist: Laura Del Fava
Illustrator: Beverley Bozarth Colgan
Page Production: Linda M. Bouchard
Prepress Coordinator: Danielle Javier
Proofreader: Alicia Eckley

Photography Credits
Cover: Margot Hartford (see pages 64–69)
Page 1: Margot Hartford (see pages 116–117)
Above: James Carrier (see pages 58–61)
Opposite, top and bottom right: Muffy Kibbey (see pages 82–83 and pages 40–41)
Opposite, bottom left: John Granen (see pages 62–63)

Abbreviations: The following abbreviations are used in the floor plans shown throughout this book.

B	Broom closet		**LR**	Living room
BR	Bedroom		**MW**	Microwave
C	Cooktop		**N**	Nook
CL	Closet		**O**	Oven
D	Dryer		**P**	Pantry
DR	Dining room		**R**	Range
DS	Desk		**R/F**	Refrigerator/Freezer
DW	Dishwasher		**S**	Sink
ES	Espresso system		**SF**	Sofa
F	Fireplace		**SH**	Shelving unit
FR	Family room		**TC**	Trash compactor
H	Hutch		**W**	Washer
HO	Home office		**WC**	Wine cooler
I	Island		**WH**	Water heater
L	Laundry		**WS**	Window seat

Recipes for Success

Who can resist a good before-and-after story? Everyone, it seems, enjoys watching a dated, dreary room turn into something special, no doubt because we see our own homes in the "befores"—and recipes for success in the "afters."

The 40 examples in this book show that today's kitchen is nothing like those of decades past. What was once a simple (and usually small) room for food preparation and casual meals now includes an array of amenities to please the serious cook, along with family-friendly features that expand the kitchen into the hub of the home. Innovations include pro-style ranges and undercabinet refrigerator and freezer drawers, while materials and components ranging from honed slate to exotic woods bring new beauty to this once-utilitarian room.

As is evident in the before-and-after floor plans, the layout of the kitchen space has also evolved. Walls have come down between the kitchen and adjoining rooms, integrating formerly separate spaces into open living areas. With expanded islands that include auxiliary appliances and secondary sinks has come an open, flexible work core.

You'll find examples of all the current trends in the following pages. Along with the floor plans, tips, and color palettes, we offer special features on notable elements of kitchen design such as storage and cabinetry.

A lot of living goes on in today's kitchen, still the most-often-remodeled room in the home. If you're ready to begin your own before-and-after makeover story, let the transformations here be your guide.

3

◀ Before | With only one north-facing window, the modest 1980s kitchen was dark and depressing. The family ate meals at a small table pushed against the wall.

Face-frame cabinets are fitted with flush-inset, Shaker-style doors and simple crown molding. This cabinet contains a surprise: a clear-glass back that affords a glimpse into adjoining rooms.

Glazed ceramic tile the color of caramel plays off warm green walls and cherrywood cabinetry. Accent tile pieces fancifully depict different vegetables.

▶ **Casement windows,** with arched divided lights and latch hardware, brighten the eating area. Cottage board (a wider version of beadboard) covers the built-in bench; the soffit above distinguishes this space from the kitchen itself.

◀ **After** | The home-owners literally followed the sun when they moved their kitchen to the west side of the house; children and guests now spill out onto the deck and into the backyard. The new eat-in kitchen accommodates a generous island and smart banquette.

▶ **Slate slab** atop the island and counters retains its natural "cleft," meaning that it's slightly textured rather than smoothly honed. Prized for its subtle color variation, this natural stone is as durable as it is handsome.

BEFORE

AFTER

Floor plans: A second-story addition made it possible to eliminate a pair of ground-level bedrooms and move the kitchen to the back of the house. The doubled area became "the new family room."

Warm walls with a slightly uneven texture bring to mind the kitchens of Tuscany.

Beveled glass in the base cabinet doors is both old-fashioned and European modern.

The honed-granite countertop on the island has a soft, matte finish. Face-frame cabinets with flush-inset doors are made of maple.

▼ Before | The product of many remodels over the years, "the kitchen that Jack built" was way beyond redemption. For the homeowners—one of them a serious amateur chef—an extensive redo was the only possible course of action.

◄ **After** │ A wood-fired pizza oven takes center stage in the stunning new kitchen. The space is every bit as hard-working as it is handsome, however: the homeowners and architect meticulously researched the options to design a room in which cooking and entertaining can occur simultaneously.

A gently bowed edge facilitates conversation among those seated at the island.

▼ **The built-in booth** offers an intimate eating area as well as a place to relax and read the morning paper. The Italian-made oven is based on a dome-shaped terra-cotta insert; it is surrounded by fireproof tiles, brick, and insulation, all covered in plaster.

Distressed pine floors lay the foundation for rich, rustic styling throughout the room.

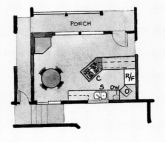

BEFORE

AFTER

Floor plans: After incorporating the existing porch area and parts of adjoining rooms, the kitchen's size grew by nearly 30 percent. Most appliances are located along the L-shaped perimeter; a second sink and dishwasher at the end of the island come in handy for large get-togethers.

▲ **Before** | The kitchen in this 1939 home was "so old and grimy we couldn't even scrub the cabinets," the homeowner lamented. The goal: to make the space clean and modern, but without moving the sink.

Custom cabinetry with fine detailing | **After** ▶ gives the new kitchen architectural "bones" and traditional charm. White ceramic subway tile on the backsplash and an ogee edging on the solid-surface countertops are classic; stainless steel appliances are a nod to the new.

Kitchen continues ▶ ▶

◀ **Removable plastic pegs** fit into perforated hardboard liners to prevent bowls, plates, and cookware from sliding around in the drawers. The perforated board can be cut to size.

▶ **Moving the range** closer to the sink results in a tighter, more efficient work core. Bar-level counters at either end of the kitchen bracket the space; near the sitting area, guests often stand at the bar and chat with the cook.

▼ **Pullout wire baskets** keep kitchen goods in order and clearly visible. You'll find lots of options in pullout units at home centers and storage specialty shops.

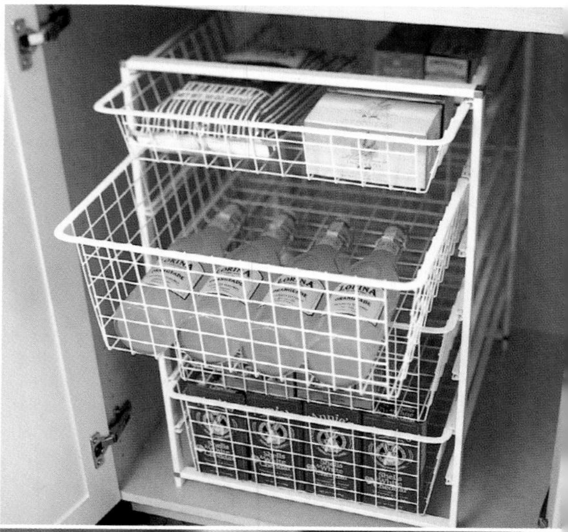

▲ **Upper cabinets** feature handsome crown molding and multipaned doors with wavy water glass; a French door with plain glass repeats the cabinets' design.

▶ **A specialized holder** mounted inside the undersink cabinet door keeps track of foil and plastic wraps.

▲ These face-frame cabinets feature flush-inset doors and drawers that fit perfectly into the openings. The door and drawer style is classic frame-and-panel.

Cabinet Basics

Cabinets typically cost more—much more—than any other part of a new kitchen, so it's important to understand your options before you purchase them. Three features define cabinets: box construction; door and drawer fit; and door and drawer style.

Box Construction

Cabinets vary in the way the cabinet "box" is put together. Think of this box as having five sides, with the front open.

Face-frame cabinets, the more traditional style, have a wood frame attached to the front edges of the box. Doors and drawers fit into the opening or cover part of it, but the frame always shows. The hinges may or may not show.

Frameless cabinets have no frame attached to the face of the box. Open the door and you see the edges of the box itself; close the door and the edges are covered. You don't see the hinges on frameless cabinets because they are attached to the inside of the door and the box (and are often called "Euro-style" hinges). Frameless cabinets can look contemporary or traditional, depending on the style of the door.

Door and Drawer Fit

Doors and drawers differ in the way they fit into or over the cabinets.

Flush-inset doors and drawers close flush with the frame on face-frame cabinets. The most traditional of door styles, this is also the most expensive, because a precise fit is required.

Partial-overlay doors and drawers cover the openings on face-frame cabinets while revealing some of the frame. Usually traditional in style, these are less expensive than flush-inset doors and drawers because there is some "play" in the fit.

Full-overlay doors and drawers cover the box completely on frameless cabinets, with just a bit of space left between the doors and drawers for clearance. They can look traditional or contemporary, depending on the style of the door.

◀ These frameless cabinets with full-overlay doors and drawers appear traditional because the door style is frame-and-panel. This combination of box construction, door fit, and door style is the most popular.

◀ Frameless, with full-overlay slab doors and drawers, these cabinets couldn't be more contemporary.

▼ The partial-overlay doors and drawers on the face-frame cabinets partly cover the box opening. The frame-and-panel doors have mitered corners where the rails and stiles meet; the drawers are slab style.

Door and Drawer Style

Doors and drawers come in two basic styles: frame-and-panel and slab. You'll often see these styles mixed in the same kitchen—typically frame-and-panel doors, but slab drawers.

Frame-and-panel doors are by far the most popular. A flat, recessed, or raised panel rests within a frame made up of two horizontal "rails" and two vertical "stiles." The popular Shaker-style variant has rails and stiles that form right-angle, rather than mitered, corners.

Slab doors can be solid wood, but they are usually made up of several layers. They're seen most frequently in contemporary settings. Slab drawers, however, can coexist nicely with frame-and-panel doors in traditional kitchens.

A cabinetry hood over the range continues the custom look.

Angled corner cabinets maximize storage above and soften the boxy lines of the kitchen. Their sides form a space for soffit lighting above the sink.

White granite tile flecked with red and black visually links the red accent wall and laminate table and the black appliances.

◄ Before | Worn vinyl flooring and yellowed oak cabinets kept this tiny U-shaped kitchen stuck in the 1950s. High on the homeowners' list of goals was a space-saving eating arrangement for four.

◄ **After** | Filled with smart storage and stylish features, the made-over kitchen delivers a compact cooking, eating, and gathering space. The existing range and refrigerator move to opposite walls in the new plan; the dishwasher also shifts, to avoid interference with the range door. The red laminate table comfortably seats the whole family.

▶ **A narrow pullout shelf unit** fits conveniently between the range and undercabinet microwave. Two-inch-square red glass tiles punch out a simple, open pattern on the porcelain tile backsplash.

— **Large, off-white porcelain floor tiles** are set on the diagonal, with a rectangular border, to visually expand the small room.

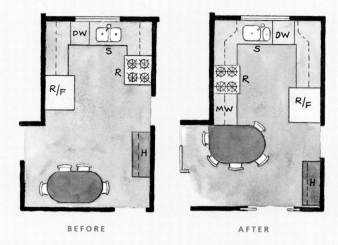

BEFORE   AFTER

Floor plans: The homeowners and kitchen designer experimented with large cardboard templates to arrive at the final tabletop shape; the opening into the family room was moved to accommodate the table.

"We worked hard to come up with a big-picture schedule that left us without a functioning kitchen for no more than six weeks. At that point things could slow down, and our lives weren't disrupted."

▲ Before | A 6-foot-wide window afforded a view of a body of water, but the glare was blinding—and the room actually looked darker because of the single light source. The vaulted ceiling, however, was a real plus.

The new design | ## After ▶

balances light, color, and texture in a marriage of modern and traditional materials. A taller, narrower over-sink window and a vertical glass-block backsplash behind the stove circulate light and minimize glare. Frameless fir cabinets are warm and textural, whereas the cool glass tile is sleek and shiny.

◄ **Wine cubbies** just to the right of the refrigerator provide dedicated storage and a welcome break in the solid-door cabinetry.

▶ **The substantial range,** backsplash, and hood offset the visual mass of the refrigerator cabinet. Additional light enters the room through a small skylight that's contiguous with the wall; glass shelves in the alcove let the light from above shine through.

▲ **Blue and black glass tiles** from 1 to 8 inches square are arranged in a stylized patchwork pattern on the backsplash. Blue-flecked granite is a natural foil for the contemporary, solid-color tile.

◄ **A 42-inch-high wall** behind the breakfast bar replaces the full wall between the kitchen and dining room, opening and linking the spaces. The new low stairwell wall (visible across the room) contributes to the sense of spaciousness.

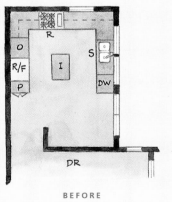

BEFORE

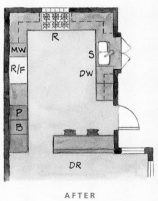

AFTER

Floor plans: An interior wall between the kitchen and dining room stood in the way of the homeowners' vision of a more unified space. Removing the wall opened and brightened the kitchen and eating area.

◂ **Before** | This condo kitchen exemplifies a poor use of limited space. The refrigerator's location rendered the end wall unusable; a tall counter was little more than a room divider and catchall surface.

An all-in-one microwave, light, and vent mounted above the range is a smart solution for cramped quarters; cubbies on either side of the unit hold cookbooks at the ready.

A gray ceramic-glass-surface cooktop with black accents coordinates with the grout, pewter hardware, and chrome faucet.

Although narrower, the new **After** ▸ galley kitchen is much more efficient. The widened peninsula provides a generous food prep area, and its 28-inch-deep base cabinets offer ample storage. Moving the refrigerator made way for upper cabinets on the end wall and a centrally located range.

▸ **Eight-inch white ceramic tile** blends seamlessly with white cabinets and a white tile-in (flush with the edge) sink; embossed accent tiles add pattern and texture to what is an otherwise smooth surface.

Fresh cabinets purchased through a home center feature a sturdy laminate finish; the gently arched panel doors are traditional.

Shelves at the end of the peninsula provide a bit of open storage and display space; gentle curves soften the corners.

Laminate flooring is durable, comfortable, and easy to care for. Its "oak" surface is actually a photographed paper layer adhered to a manufactured core and sealed against wear.

▼ Before

The kitchen was dreary and boxlike, with a tiny table crammed into one corner. An add-on aluminum bay window overlooking the backyard was out of sync with the traditional style of the 1919 home's exterior.

After ▶

European styling shines in every aspect of the transformed kitchen. Multicolored solid-surface countertops play off a bold backsplash composed of hand-made ³⁄₈-inch glass tile. Solid maple cabinets are simply styled to showcase the wood's luminous grain.

Kitchen continues ▶ ▶

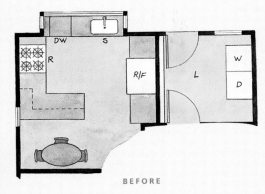

◄ **A built-in espresso system** is a key element of the kitchen's modern design. No plumbing is involved; cold water goes into a reservoir, just as it does with a typical countertop coffeemaker.

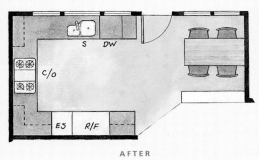

BEFORE

AFTER

Floor plans:
Removing the wall between the kitchen and laundry and reconfiguring the perimeter cabinets created a room that's spacious and functional (a small laundry area was built in elsewhere). Additional windows along the exterior wall admit soft light.

▲ **Nature's colors** inspired a malachite green, Murano glass–tile backsplash. The terrazzo countertop, custom designed to complement the backsplash, is made from concrete and ground-up glass from curbside and industrial recycling sources. (This heavy material requires solid wood cabinets for support.)

◄ **A minimalist wall hood** consisting of a stainless steel "chimney" and glass canopy allows a nearly unimpeded view of the counter-to-ceiling back-splash. Between the gas/electric cooktop and the electric oven is a handy utensil drawer.

▶ **Two casement windows** were chosen for the eating area, rather than one large one, to harmonize with the proportions of windows throughout the home. A single-pane French door expands the view and grants access to the backyard.

Carrara marble on the countertops and backsplash is the perfect pattern-and-texture foil for plain painted cabinetry.

Reeded glass in the upper cabinets is a tailored touch.

Walnut-stained birch distinguishes the surface of the breakfast bar topping the half-wall.

◄Before | A redo of this 1926 Tudor-style cottage was not for the fainthearted: "It had been unoccupied for seven years," said the homeowner/architect. Despite a leaky roof and termites, its potential was clear to him and to his wife, an interior designer.

After | Originally

remodeled to sell, the house is now happily inhabited by its designers. "We planned a kitchen that would appeal to everyone, and it has turned out to be better than any we've lived in." Technically a galley, the kitchen maintains a close relationship to the family room across a half-wall separating the two.

Beadboard paneling is right at home with period architecture that's been fitted with fresh fixtures and materials.

▶ **The glass-front cabinets** are everyone's favorite feature because their lower-than-usual shelves afford quick access to items used every day. A farmhouse-style sink and white cabinets with pewter-finish hardware preserve the home's vintage character.

BEFORE   AFTER

Floor plans: When this house was built, a kitchen was no more than a place in which to work. In the whole-house revival, the new kitchen blends into the family room at the back of the house; the dining room now occupies the area of the original kitchen.

NOTES FROM THE ARCHITECT

"We toyed with having an island, but we went with a peninsula instead because it gives us more counter space. The half-wall on the outside of the peninsula makes for a cleaner view from the family room."

Before | The makeover plan for this ranch-house kitchen was modest, but it quickly grew. "We just wanted to change the cooktop and reface the cabinets," explained one of the homeowners. "We ended up ripping the room down to the studs."

8.19.02

Entertaining is | **After** ▶ easier than ever in this warm, welcoming space, with one hitch: "Now we have to drag people from the kitchen into the dining room. No one wants to leave." L-shaped peninsulas increase counter space while keeping the work core open.

Kitchen continues ▶ ▶

▶ **Black granite tiles** 12 inches square are set "on point" to comprise a bold backsplash behind the six-burner cooktop. A honed surface gives the tiles their elegant matte finish.

◀ **An undercounter refrigerator and wine cooler** in the pantry hold beverages for entertaining and everyday needs. "Quilted" glass in the upper cabinets gives the pantry its own design identity.

▲ **For the walk-in pantry,** the homeowners economized by choosing cabinets from a discount home furnishings store. A pullout unit delivers ample space for nonperishables.

◀ **A prep sink** at the breakfast bar counter comes in handy when both cooks are in the kitchen; the gooseneck faucet with brushed-chrome finish matches the cabinetry hardware. Reeded glass in the cabinet doors adds yet another texture to the scheme.

Kitchen continues ▶ ▶

Floor plans: Standard-width openings into the living and dining rooms made the original kitchen and eating area feel closed off from the rest of the house. Widening them enhanced the flow from room to room.

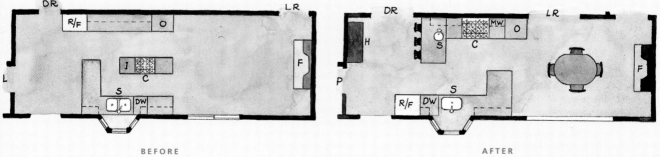

BEFORE

AFTER

◄ **In the eating area,** the ambience is one of casual elegance: black granite tiles and charcoal gray plaster recall the cooktop's backsplash and hood. The sleek mantel is made of mahogany.

► **In a bid for simplicity,** the homeowners chose to eliminate the standard backsplash. Without it the room feels lighter, and more of the warm wall color shows.

▲ **Honed granite** in shades of cabernet and saffron flecked with black links the wood tones with the black accents used throughout the room.

► **Display shelves** in the base cabinets facing the fireplace help provide a psychological transition from kitchen to eating area. A floating floor of cork topped by a thin veneer of mahogany is comfortable underfoot and easy to maintain.

With the exposed sinks **Before** ▶
far from the appliances and a water heater
out in the open, this turn-of-the-century
kitchen was unsightly, inconvenient, and
long overdue for a major renovation.

A passion for their old **After** ▶
house was the driving force behind
the homeowners' ambitious makeover.
With the help of a kitchen designer,
they transformed the disjointed space
into a room loaded with traditional
charm and modern appliances.

◀ **Four-inch-square ceramic tile** covers the countertops
and backsplash in cheerful color; shamrock green V-cap
edging and slender liner pieces accent the expanse of
bright yellow. The vintage-style range hood consists of
beadboard and tile over a metal liner.

Floor plans: An addition on two sides of
the house provided extra space for the
new kitchen and a home office. Appliances
ganged on adjoining walls deliver an organized work core; the new laundry room and
bath are now conveniently situated.

BEFORE

AFTER

A tall, shallow pantry makes use of a slice of wasted space where a wall juts into the kitchen from the next room.

Slender columns and a half-wall below do the job of the former load-bearing wall; shallow cabinets on the other side hold kids' books and craft supplies.

A warm green on the cabinets is the perfect color companion for the sunny yellow tile.

The 1950s-era dinette set, a relic from the husband's childhood, was a "must-keep" item for the new kitchen.

◄Before | As was typical of early-20th-century kitchens, this was never meant to be a gathering place. Dark cabinets from a 1970s remodel and four separate doorways gave the space its tired, fragmented look.

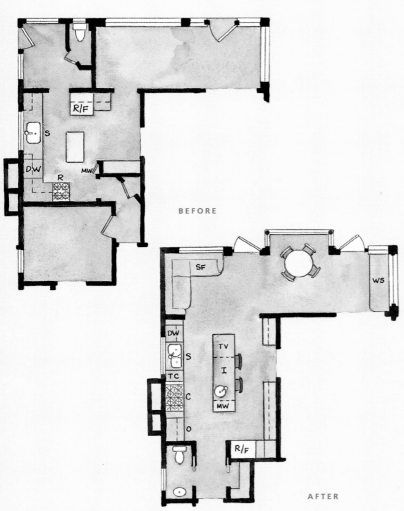

BEFORE

AFTER

Floor plans: The architect claimed 4 feet from an adjacent hall and bedroom to expand the kitchen. Where walls and a powder room once blocked the view to the garden, an open family room and eating area now runs the width of the house.

▼ After

A "family-room feel" to the kitchen and a strong visual connection to the garden were the homeowners' greatest desires. Craftsman design elements stay true to the architecture of the house, while contemporary materials and sunny colors bring the space into today's world.

Kitchen continues ▶ ▶

LESSONS FROM THE HOMEOWNERS

"We learned that many heads are better than one," the homeowners said.
"Meeting weekly with the entire team helped everyone know who was doing what and when.
That kind of clarity kept the project moving along beautifully."

◄ **Twelve-inch-square glass tiles** in terra-cotta, sunny yellow, and sage green form a bold harlequin pattern on the backsplash. Seventeen-inch-square concrete floor tiles in a paler terra-cotta and oatmeal are quiet by comparison. Bar stools fit the knee space under the granite-topped island.

► **A casual dining table** between the window seat and sofa takes advantage of the view and the natural light; the decorative pendant light with an amber beaded-glass shade distinguishes the eating area.

▼ **To the left of the stainless steel refrigerator** is a narrow broom closet, with interior hooks for hanging cleaning tools, and a small appliance garage.

◄ **A tambour door** at the end of the island conceals a TV perfectly situated for viewing from the sofa.

▲ **Recessed panels** on doors and drawers are outlined with a simple bead, a quintessentially Craftsman detail; the frameless cabinet construction is thoroughly modern.

39

Before | The high ceilings in this older home suggested lots of design potential for the kitchen—none of which had been realized. An add-on greenhouse window from the recent past was a "must-go" feature.

Soapstone countertops are impervious to damage; the matching backsplash is embellished with reproduction deco tiles.

With minimal changes to the **After** ▶ footprint, the homeowner/designer created a sleek, sophisticated kitchen that capitalizes on the existing space and soaring ceiling. Fir cabinets are tall and roomy; refrigerator and freezer drawers to the right of the sink conserve floor space.

Floor plans: A brick chimney behind the range ate up valuable square footage; eliminating it and the adjacent wall expanded the center of the room. On a nearby wall, a freestanding buffet replaces a bank of tall cabinets.

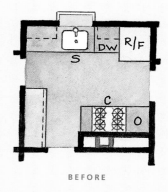

BEFORE

AFTER

Side panels on the upper cabinets are fitted with glass so light coming through the window fills the cabinets.

Dark-stained crown molding matches trim in the rest of the home.

Mounting the faucet on the wall keeps the space behind the sink clean and simple.

▶ **A crackle-glaze, ceramic-tile backsplash** complements pale yellow Venetian plaster walls. The backsplash niche holds cooking oils; wall niches for knives and utensils are lined with pounded copper. A base-level refrigerator to the left of the range is topped with butcher block, serving two purposes.

A slim vertical cabinet to the right of the freezer drawer stores cookie sheets and pizza stones upright.

41

▲**Before** | As is typical of turn-of-the-century Victorian homes, the original kitchen was just an empty room, with the sink relegated to a separate annex. Needless to say, it was an inconvenient setup. A tall cabinet was the only built-in.

The homeowners | **After** ▶ came to the project with a clear vision: "We wanted our new kitchen to look like a true Victorian, without compromising our ability to live and work in it." To achieve vintage charm with modern function, they chose state-of-the-art components designed, whenever possible, in the Victorian vernacular.

Kitchen continues ▶ ▶

◀ **The homeowners chose stainless steel** for the main countertops and integral sink over more expensive solid surfacing or stone, preferring to put their remodeling dollars into the cabinets. Seen through the sliding windows above the sink is the new living room.

▶ **Extra-deep cabinets** were specified to be flush with the standard-depth refrigerator. This trick gave the appliance the look of an expensive counter-depth (shallower) model.

▲ **A Carrara marble countertop** on the island, 1¼ inches thick, has a flat profile with an eased (slightly rounded) edge. The gooseneck faucet is polished chrome; the small black switch governs the garbage disposer.

◀ **Open drawers** with hand cutouts in place of hardware allow the smoothest access to pots and pans stowed beneath the cooktop.

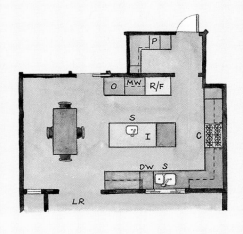

BEFORE

AFTER

Floor plans: The wall separating a small bedroom from the kitchen came down, and 4 feet were added to the back of the house. These two moves made room for a generous kitchen, open breakfast area, and adjoining new living room.

Kitchen continues ▶ ▶

◀ **Victorian charm** inhabits the "back pantry," with its tall doors concealing modern pullouts, boxy drawers, and V-groove paneling behind open shelves.

▼ **V-groove paneling** recessed into rail-and-stile doors and drawers is quintessentially Victorian. (V-groove differs from beadboard, which has a rounded "bead" running down the groove.) Plug molding installed just under the countertop is painted to match.

Color Palette

The muted blue-green on the cabinets was often used in Victorian-era solariums. Because it is nearly neutral, the color works equally well with stainless steel and gray-veined marble. A creamy white for the walls is a suitable companion color.

▲ **Sheet linoleum** cut into 12-inch-wide strips makes for a floor bold in scale yet subtle in color. Composed mainly of ground wood and cork that is bound by resins, linoleum is resilient and long wearing.

◀ **A butcher-block section** at one end of the furniture-style island is just the spot to roll out pastry or prep vegetables. The open shelf below provides visual relief in the large unit.

▲ Pullout pantry units in these custom cabinets consist of narrow vertical glide-outs with adjustable-height shelves. For easy filling and retrieval, locate pullouts close to counters where you unload groceries or prepare food.

▼ Laminated glass (see page 76) is a good choice for a pantry in a great-room location; sliding cabinet doors don't interrupt the flow of traffic.

Pantry Particulars

Pantries are staging a strong comeback in today's kitchen. Hectic lifestyles encourage bulk buying at warehouse and discount stores, and a growing interest in multiethnic cooking fuels the desire for specialty ingredients. There's no doubt about it: everyone needs more space for varied food-stuffs, specialized appliances, and exotic tools. Fortunately, there's room in every kitchen for some version of a pantry. Here are four choices:

■ Pullout pantry units, by far the most popular option, are available for almost all new cabinetry, whether stock or custom. They're also made to fit existing cabinets; check out home centers and storage specialty shops, and be sure to measure carefully before buying.

■ A closet pantry, consisting of shelving installed in an existing closet, is a relatively easy retrofit. Shelves can be as shallow as 4 inches (for canned food) or as deep as 12 inches (for boxed cereals). All-the-way-up shelves are great for bulky but lightweight items such as paper goods.

■ A walk-in pantry is the ultimate in kitchen storage. A walk-in may include cabinets with doors and drawers, open shelves, a work counter, and even a desk. Larger pantries often contain a broom closet as well.

■ A butler's pantry, traditionally a staging area for meal presentation and a repository for dishware, is a walk-in pantry with any or all of the following: sink, bar, wine cooler, microwave, and refrigerator. Typically, its cabinets are nicely finished, because the room can be seen from the kitchen or dining room.

▲ Glass-front drawers for grains and pasta, narrow cubbies for platters, and open shelving for everything else maintain a cozy sense of order in this walk-in pantry.

▶ The exterior window and decorative glass fronts on the compartments lend a light and airy look to this butler's pantry. The mirrored backsplash also helps make this small space feel larger.

◀ Wraparound shelving turns an existing closet off the kitchen into a much-needed pantry. A glass-front door lets in the light and makes the tiny kitchen appear larger.

◂ Before
Barely 300 square feet in area, the former kitchen was essentially a corridor between the living room and a small breakfast area. An interior wall concealed a stairway.

▼ **After** | Shifting all appliances to the exterior walls allowed for an open stairway, increasing the sense of space and creating a bridge between the new kitchen and living room. Mahogany-and-metal railings have a strong yet airy architectural presence.

▶ **An angled mahogany table** elegantly marks the imaginary divide between kitchen and living room.

▶ **Frameless beechwood cabinets** feature full-overlay doors. On the upper cabinets flanking the range, laminated-glass doors (see page 76) perch on stainless steel supports attached to each cabinet's box. Highly patterned granite on the counters and backsplash injects curves into the angular scheme; its honed finish is matte rather than shiny.

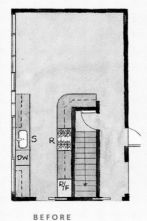

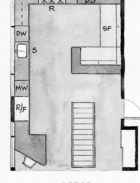

BEFORE

AFTER

Floor plans: The kitchen now extends into what was the breakfast room. An L-shaped work core lets the cook work while family and friends congregate in the sitting area, with its built-in sofa and desk.

51

▲ Before | A typical
kitchen in a 1923 bungalow
lacked almost everything the
homeowners wanted—chief
among them, light, space, and
modern amenities.

Without adding | # After ▶
a single square foot, the archi-
tect/homeowner stayed true
to tradition while creating
a kitchen that's convenient
and efficient. Cottage board
topped by a plate rail forms a
1920s-style backsplash; white
frameless cabinets with full-
overlay doors store up-to-date
kitchenware.

Kitchen continues ▶ ▶

Adding on to a home is always expensive, but, counsels the homeowner/architect, "if you can stay within the exterior structure while removing interior walls to increase square footage, you'll significantly contain costs."

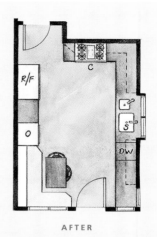

◀ **To balance the light** from the banquette windows and back door, as well as to maximize the garden view below, the window opening was lengthened and the sill eliminated. The casement windows close directly against the countertop.

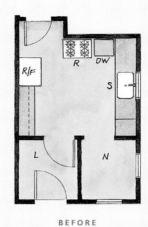

BEFORE AFTER

Floor plans: A tiny utility room off the kitchen and a 6-by-6-foot breakfast nook were too small to be useful. Removing the interior walls and reconfiguring windows and doors garnered both space and light.

▲ **A narrow granite counter** between the ovens (on the left) and the refrigerator provides breathing space in a solid wall of appliances and cabinetry; it's also the perfect venue for the homeowner's garden-grown flowers.

◀ **The gently pointed arch** on the open bookcase was inspired by a breakfront in the dining room. Behind the pillows, the back of the banquette wraps around the corner for a smooth transition.

▶ **For design continuity** the backsplash pattern repeats, in different proportions, the surround of the living room's fireplace. The 12-by-12-inch limestone tiles were cut to fit the space.

▲ Before | This kitchen's assets—well-constructed cabinets, vintage tile, and hardwood floors—were masked by layers of worn paint, aged grout, and scuffed linoleum. Nothing had been touched since 1948.

A tailored Roman shade replaces the original scalloped-wood valance for a sleek, simple window treatment. Black banding on the shade's edges subtly repeats the black bullnose (rounded-edge) trim on the original tile.

▼ **A porthole door** dreamed up by the homeowner/designer leads to his home office.

Pristine white grout replaces dingy old grout; buttery yellow and black tile was cleaned, buffed, and sealed for a bright, fresh look.

▼ After

Adding a multipurpose island solves a major problem in the original layout: the stove blocked a door and was too far from the sink. The island, which houses a cooktop, oven, and prep area, brings the appliances closer to the sink; its generous overhang also accommodates bar stools.

Old cabinets get a face-lift with white marine (waterproof) paint. To achieve this lacquerlike finish, free of brushstrokes, the homeowner removed the doors and applied paint to them and to the cabinet interiors with a sprayer.

A stainless steel top and high-gloss auto body paint make the island a handsome focal point.

Kitchen continues ▶▶

▼**Before** | Gypsum-board arches partly covered the windows of this 1929 Spanish Colonial Revival–style bungalow. A stairway from the back of the kitchen to the garage level cut off access to the outdoors.

Suffused with | **After** ▶ light throughout the day, the bright and airy kitchen is now a favorite gathering place for family and guests. The fake arches went first; then two original steel-sash windows were welded to make one larger window over the sink. A butcher-block surface over-hangs the island on three sides, allowing seating and room for two cooks.

LESSONS FROM THE HOMEOWNERS

"We wanted a light, airy kitchen, but we were determined to preserve the architectural integrity of this little Spanish casita. When you remodel the kitchen in a house of an earlier era, be prepared to do the footwork necessary to find the appropriate materials. If you don't, you'll end up with a kitchen that's not in sync with the architecture of the home."

▼ **Glass-front cabinets** with beadboard backs showcase the homeowner's collection of Bauer and Fiesta dishware. Inside, 3-inch recessed halogen lights illuminate the display.

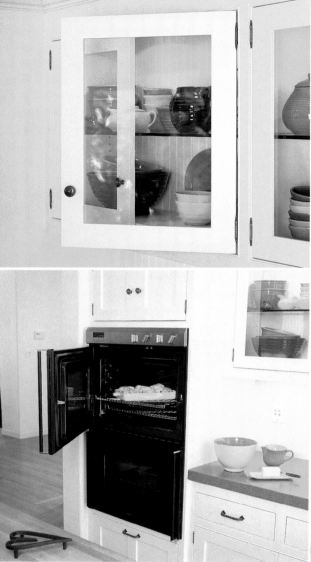

▲ **Side-opening oven doors** are a good choice where tight space precludes the more usual bottom-hinged style.

▶ **Custom-made ceramic field tile** was matched to the white of the cabinets. On the accent tiles, the glaze was rubbed off to reveal a base color similar to that of the integral-color concrete counter.

◀ **The white apron-front farmhouse sink,** beadboard, and face-frame cabinets with flush-inset doors and drawers are true to the era; stained beams, hardwood floors, and pewter hardware evoke the robust charm of Santa Barbara, California, style.

▶ **A divided drawer** keeps cutting boards both separated and accessible.

▲ **Drawers of different depths** under the cooktop prevent the usual jumble of cookware in a base cabinet.

◀ **Pendant fixtures** with pewter-and-glass shades wash the island in soft light. A tall pantry and broom closet utilize often-ignored corner space; French doors with horizontal lights replicate the original window style.

Floor plans: Moving the staircase to a more central location, near the home's entry, made room for an 8-by-10-foot deck accessible through French doors. A central island multiplied the space for food preparation and social gatherings.

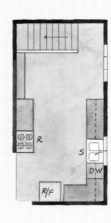

BEFORE

AFTER

The new island is topped with laminated maple, a surface suitable for food prep or casual meals.

◂ Before | Dark walnut cabinetry, "harvest gold" countertops, and tiny windows—all the signatures of a 1970s remodel—gave this 1906 house its "Addams Family" ambience.

The V-groove backsplash was custom milled from whole sections of MDF (medium-density fiberboard) for precision spacing and seamless panels.

◄ After | Clean, simple lines and today's colors brighten the new kitchen while respecting the home's traditional architecture. Face-frame cabinets with flush-inset doors are classic; the countertops, made of paper fibers strengthened with resins, are scratch, stain, and heat resistant.

A built-in bench with V-groove paneling on its back and sides benefits from natural light in the eating nook.

▶ **Stainless steel radiator screens** make eye-catching (and air-circulating) inserts for cabinet doors. A sloping drainboard recessed into the countertop is another nod to practicalities of the past.

Color Palette

Sophisticated yet playful, the color scheme offers an unexpected range of hues for painted surfaces; bright "marigold" and "tomato" are intense accents.

BEFORE

AFTER

Floor plans: The location of the powder room, between the kitchen and the nook, couldn't have been worse. Moving it, and condensing the back staircase, enlarged and unified the kitchen and eating area.

▲ Before | Light, airy—
and outdated—the existing kitchen had two features the homeowner wished to repeat or keep: sandblasted glass in the over-sink windows, for privacy, and a trio of handblown glass pendants above the island.

The homeowner's | ## After ▶
passion for glass is reflected throughout the new space— on the backsplash and island counter, in the upper cabinet doors, narrow "sill" shelf, and updated windows. A tight work core renders the space as practical as it is stunning.

Kitchen continues ▶ ▶

◀ A glass shelf relates to the window above it and the glass tile backsplash below it. Along its back edge, the shelf is fitted with ¾-inch-wide light tape, hardwired and dimmable, to illuminate the sink and countertop at night.

▶ Handsome cabinets made of anagré, a hardwood native to Africa, and finished with high-gloss lacquer introduce strong visual texture to the overall design. An angled pantry adjoins the paneled refrigerator. The microwave is stowed in the eye-level cabinet with front-lifting door to the right of the refrigerator.

▲ A thick slab of Onami glass, a variation on traditional Victorian glue-chipped glass, contributes a swirling, wavelike texture to the island. To achieve the pattern, cowhide glue is applied to one side of the glass: as it dries, the glass chips, while the flip side remains smooth.

◀ The placement of the lower oven—on the inner side of the island—allows for an unbroken line of cabinetry against the wall. Pedestals support the cast-glass countertop just above the oven, creating a unique under-counter display area.

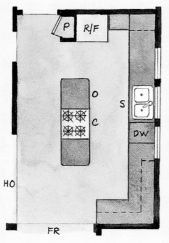

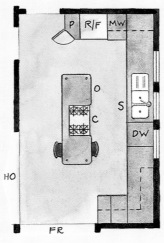

Floor plans: At first glance, the new kitchen's footprint is close to the old one's, but a host of changes—subtle and bold—in surfaces and components adds up to a complete makeover.

Kitchen continues ▶ ▶

◀ **Art-glass pieces** on display in the adjoining family room establish the palette for colorful furnishings and other art. A custom-designed area rug pulls it all together.

▶ **A swivel-and-glide shelf system** makes the most of a corner cabinet. The pull-out door is fitted with attached shelves; as the door swivels out, additional shelves glide from the interior corner to the cabinet opening.

▲ **Celadon glass tile** was custom sized to fit the backsplash; matching covers minimize the receptacles. Deep greens in the Guatemalan-marble countertop make subtle reference to the backsplash and island counter.

▶ **Inlaid squares of walnut** punctuate the ash flooring and repeat the square motif of the sink windows. A natural finish preserves the woods' intrinsic colors.

Before

A non-load-bearing post and a small buffet counter contributed to the closed-in feeling of this 1950s Eichler-designed tract house. The owners hoped to simplify and streamline the kitchen without significantly altering the floor plan.

After

Eliminating the counter and post between the kitchen and living area opened the space and made room for a built-in breakfast table for two. More light, new appliances, and a richer color palette bring the kitchen up to date while preserving its mid-century modernist character.

▼ **Plywood cabinets** *(left)* stained palomino and russet red accentuate the clean lines of Eichler design.
A new window *(right)* with a commercial-grade aluminum frame extends from the backsplash to the ceiling. The seamless stainless steel sink includes an apron edge.

The architectural bones of the home are emphasized by dark purple paint on the beams and posts.

Catching the light are various stainless steel components: hood, range backsplash, sink, and hardware.

Undercabinet strip lights supplement the pendant globes original to the home.

Glass ties it all together: etched glass on this breakfast counter and in the upper cabinet doors, green wire glass (similar to old-fashioned, diamond-patterned safety glass) on the backsplash.

Before | A 1980s

kitchen with dark-grouted tile, bright yellow walls, and passé oak cabinets was ripe for renewal; black appliances were in good condition but looked out of place among the light surfaces.

"Industrial" | After ▶

materials—steel, concrete, acrylic, and glass—combine with natural elements and neutral colors for a bold transformation. Metal panels attached to cabinet doors and concrete smoothed over the tile countertops blend better with the dark appliances.

Kitchen continues ▶ ▶

◄ **Galvanized steel panels** washed in muriatic acid add structural interest to the cabinets. The panels are first glued to the doors and drawers and then attached with black-painted screws; wrought-iron handles are attached with bolts.

► **A massive dining table** constructed of rough-hewn oiled incense cedar has the visual presence to fill—but not crowd—the space.

▼ **An innovative chandelier** made of acrylic plastic and airline cable sets a mood of futuristic elegance in the eating area.

▲ **An inexpensive utility cart,** painted black and topped with butcher block, becomes a "bonus counter." Hanging pots and pans make best use of the space below the butcher block.

► **Concrete countertops** are a popular choice for their substantial good looks and durability. In this case, the existing tile surface was prepped and coated with several layers of concrete specially mixed for countertops.

Glass Act

Everyone dreaming of a new kitchen visualizes handsome cabinets and spiffy appliances . . . usually in the context of an ideal layout. But other elements add to the enjoyment of your new kitchen, too. Glass is one such element. As manufacturers create better and more varied products, the decorative and practical potential of this material deserves a closer look. Here are six popular options.

- Satin-etched glass, sometimes called "frosted" glass, has been chemically treated on the back side for a soft, ethereal effect.

- Laminated glass has a layer of transparent or opaque film sandwiched between two pieces of clear glass. Smooth on both sides, it's ideal for areas where fingerprints are an issue.

- Glass block, widely popular in the 1940s and 1950s, now comes in different surface textures and various sizes (the most typical being 8 inches square and 4 inches deep).

- Seeded glass has tiny, randomly scattered bubbles on one side that catch light and gently soften an interior view.

- Reeded glass, also called ribbed glass, features vertical ridges that refract the light uniformly for an even diffusion and moderate blurring of a cabinet's contents.

- "New antique" is an oft-used term for patterned glass that looks old.

▲ Seeded glass is ideally suited to cabinets with interior lighting, which picks out its bubbles and makes them sparkle.

▼ Laminated glass in both the fronts and backs of upper cabinets veils the view of the house next door, while clear glass in the backsplash area captures light from a narrow side yard.

▼ Patterned panes, though new, have the look of antique German glass. They offer just enough wavy pattern to make simple cabinets interesting, and can lend an air of authenticity to a period kitchen remodel.

▲ Glass block in this soaring backsplash sheds light on what's cooking while reducing glare (see pages 16–19). Sealed mortar between the blocks makes the surface durable and easy to clean.

◄ Satin-etched glass is a lighter, less expensive alternative to laminated glass for locations where splashes and spills are not a real worry.

► Reeded-glass doors on a two-part appliance garage add depth and openness to upper cabinetry. Because of its sturdiness, reeded glass is a good choice for flip-ups and other doors that see a lot of action.

▲ Before | At first

glance the intense blue tile, garish carpet, and prominently grained cabinets are the main offenders in this kitchen... but the real problem was an inefficient layout that also squandered a fantastic view.

"I'm a family | ## After ▶

cook," says the homeowner and mother of three active boys, "and I wanted a kitchen that works for me every day." White appliances, birch cabinetry, and granite countertops are in sync with that spirit. Everyone's favorite spot? The banquette, where—for now, at least—this family of five can eat together.

Kitchen continues ▶▶

◄ **A butcher-block counter** between the prep sink and range lets the homeowner wash, chop, and cook without ever dripping on the floor. Tumbled-marble tiles of various sizes make up the backsplash; resin receptacle covers to match cost much less than marble ones.

▶ **Thirty-inch-deep cabinetry** gives the standard refrigerator the appearance of a built-in. Partial-overlay doors on face-frame cabinets sport beadboard panels and satin nickel pulls and knobs.

▼ **The homeowners' research** paid off in the details, such as a wood heat vent that blends with the base of the banquette.

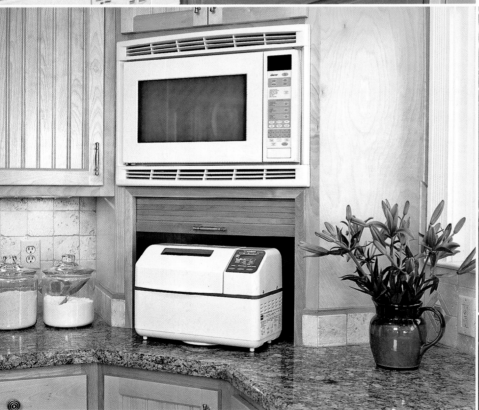

▲ **The appliance garage** is tall enough to comfortably house the bread maker. Because the base cabinets are 6 inches deeper than usual, the cook can simply pull each appliance forward and use it right in place.

▶ **Undercabinet lights** illuminate the alcove and granite countertop on the built-in hutch; glass-front doors reveal the top-lit contents.

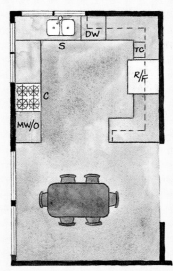

BEFORE

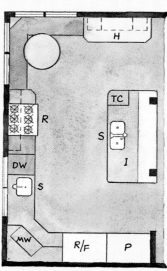

AFTER

Floor plans: Cut off from the living room by a wall and cabinets, the original kitchen was closed in and congested, whereas the adjacent eating area had space to spare. Removing a wall, gutting the kitchen, and relocating the dining area made way for an island, banquette, and hutch.

▲ Before

Last "refreshed" in the 1980s, this kitchen had a split personality, according to the new homeowner: "On one side it was Grandma's kitchen, and on the other side it had a commercial range and restaurant shelf."

Markedly | ## After ▶

more efficient, the new kitchen boasts more work surfaces and storage on both sides of the divide. The biggest and best change: installing new windows higher on the wall, clearing the way for a longer countertop, wine cubbies, and a small writing station.

The subway-tile backsplash repeats the wall color as well as the horizontal lines of the windows, for a cohesive effect.

Pale green solid-surface countertops, though not true to the era of this older home, suit the young family's active lifestyle.

Three-inch-wide wainscoting varies in height, rising to meet the windowsills and, in the far corner, the small display shelf.

▶ **The existing range,** now outlined in green tile trim pieces, is right at home in the new layout; a custom hood vents through the wall and then up to avoid the ceiling beam. Unmatched cabinet styles on either side of the range keep the look eclectic and casual.

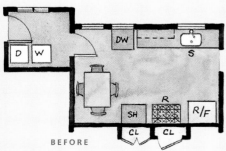

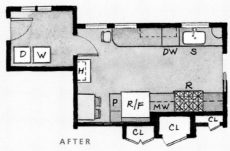

BEFORE

AFTER

Floor plans: Space borrowed from the kitchen is added to closets located in the adjacent hallway. Reversing the swing on the door to the outside makes doing the laundry easier.

▲ Before | The kitchen in this Victorian home had next to no counter space but plenty of doors—to the hall, dining room, and downstairs. The appliances were so old that no new models would fit into the existing cabinets. A total reconfiguration was in order.

Warm and | **After ▶** elegant, the new kitchen reflects the homeowner's love of antique detailing... and devotion to Internet auction sites. Vintage leaded glass, lighting fixtures, and hardware were all purchased there. New components— including the cherry-and-granite island, enameled hood, and face-frame cabinetry—have period styling.

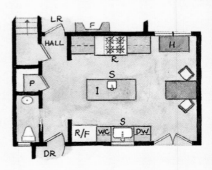

Floor plans: Pushing out the kitchen meant moving the existing hall to the opposite side of the house and eliminating most of the deck. A wide opening connects the new hall and kitchen.

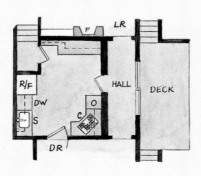

BEFORE

AFTER

Kitchen continues ►►

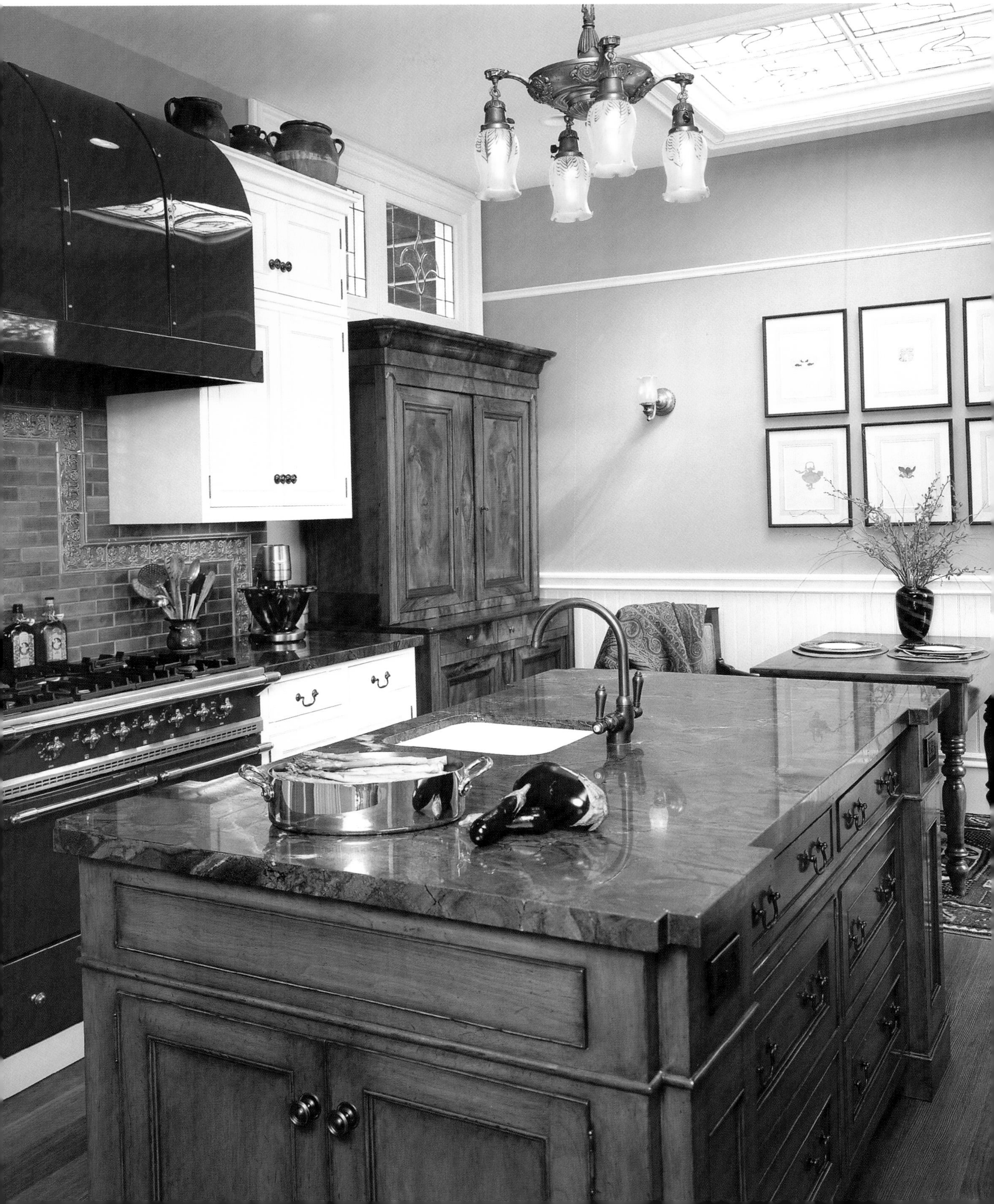

When it comes to choosing materials, the homeowner counsels following your heart: "It's the labor that's so expensive, so you might as well buy the materials you love and do things the way you want from the start. If you decide to do something over, you'll be paying for the labor twice."

▼ **A slotted drawer** keeps lids from shifting in the base cabinet. Other drawers have red laminate bottoms to match the range.

▼ **Wood dowels** inserted into the bottom of a cupboard drawer organize and protect china.

▲ **The owner's prized** French walnut cupboard, circa 1830, was destined for a prominent place as a hutch in the new kitchen. Its handsome proportions and warm tones were copied in the built-to-spec island.

◀ **A blend of beauty and utility,** painted cabinets with flush-inset doors incorporate details common to 18th- and 19th-century French and English furniture; dishwasher drawers to the left of the sink are up-to-the-minute yet look traditional. Ceramic subway tile and a fireclay sink with brass faucet add to the yesteryear ambience.

▶ **French doors** that open onto a remaining section of deck were fitted with some of the antique leaded glass used throughout the room; new transom windows were made to match. Authentic Victorian sconces cast soft light on an old French farm table.

Dark gray countertops are made of *pietra grigia*, an Italian slate that looks like dark limestone but is as dense and durable as granite.

◀ Before

Despite its light paintwork, skylight, and clerestory windows, the owners of this 1960s home experienced their kitchen as "dark and enclosed." Their desire for an expansive, unified layout and their preference for modernist design motivated the makeover plan.

◄After | The load-bearing wall between the kitchen and living room was replaced with a structure-reinforcing frame running the length of the kitchen. Painted a rich red, the frame contributes architectural drama to the new open plan.

Sleek cabinets of anagré wood are a natural foil for steel and slate.

A frameless-mirror backsplash bounces light around and also implies a larger space behind and beyond the cabinets.

The upper ledge running the length of the sink countertop helps protect the mirror from splashing water and provides "wall space" for receptacles.

▼ **Open above and below** to the adjoining hallway, the upper cabinets at the end of the kitchen appear to float. The cooktop over a separate oven, rather than a more traditional range, maintains the clean, unbroken edge on the inside of the island. The configuration is practical as well: the appliances can be of different sizes or powered by different energy sources.

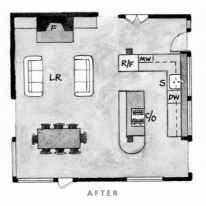

Floor plans: Extending the perimeter cabinets into the former dining area and adding an island unite the kitchen with the living and dining space.

BEFORE

AFTER

▲ Before
A standard 8-foot ceiling, along with a narrow doorway into the dining room, made this 1940s ranch-style home's kitchen feel cramped. Behind the white doors was an inadequate pantry.

After ▶
A vaulted ceiling transformed the space without changing the perimeter—thereby containing the cost. The large island provides deep storage and doubles as a buffet for entertaining. Maple cabinets join concrete countertops in a harmony of traditional and innovative materials.

Kitchen continues ▶ ▶

◄ **A change in the floor plan** made room for a narrow hutch. In the far corner is the cooktop, with a pop-up, downdraft vent. The homeowner decided against an island cooktop, to avoid a view-blocking hood, and the home's concrete foundation ruled out venting through the floor.

► **Stainless steel appliances** are teamed with warm-toned cabinetry and cool-colored concrete. Stainless knobs and pulls, plus pieces from the homeowner's collection of utilitarian metal objects, help blend these materials.

DESIGN TIP

A good spot for a microwave is under the island, because many models are deeper than standard wall cabinets.

► **The tall pantry and broom closet** compensate for limited upper-cabinet storage on the window wall. Glass-front compartments above, which hold occasional-use items, keep the unit from looking top-heavy.

► **Base cabinets on the island** are fitted with wire-reinforced, sandblasted safety glass and brushed–stainless steel pulls. Safety glass is a good choice for lower cabinet doors, while from an aesthetic perspective, obscuring glass blurs the contents and softens the view from the dining room.

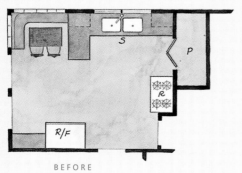

BEFORE

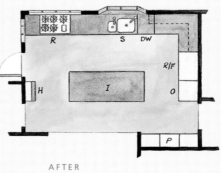

AFTER

Floor plans: The new 9-foot opening between kitchen and dining room makes the two rooms feel like one. Space borrowed from the garage becomes a 6-foot-wide, 18-inch-deep combined pantry and broom closet.

Island Attractions

Islands have been a staple of kitchen design for decades, valued for both their versatility and their good looks. Expanded functions and innovative accoutrements dazzle today's homeowners and kitchen planners alike. Consider the long list of island pluses:

■ Most islands can accommodate more than one worker, a real boon to multiple-cook families.

■ Islands "direct traffic" in a kitchen, steering visitors and after-school munchers away from and around the work core.

■ Besides offering more surface area on which to prepare food, the bonus territory can become a casual dining spot, homework station, or party buffet.

■ An island is a great spot to simply hang out and, though we may not care to admit it, makes a useful catch-all surface for the day's mail, notes, and schoolbooks.

■ Under-island storage frees up counter space and can reduce the number of upper cabinets on the kitchen perimeter, resulting in a more open look.

■ Built-in appliance options are growing, from the standard cooktops and prep sinks to compost bins, warming ovens, and refrigerator drawers.

▲ This simple island was constructed from two stock cabinets to match perimeter cabinets. Beadboard paneling was applied to what were the backs and sides of the stock cabinets; doors and drawers are on the far sides.

▶ Solid maple cabinets form the base of this centerpiece island. White marble meets charcoal honed limestone in the fanciful curved countertop. An electric cooking element (with its matching vessel) installed in the countertop as well as a warming oven underneath enhance the island's function.

▼ Cherry-stained cabinetry and red-streaked granite combine to give a fine-furniture look to this handsome island. The butcher-block cart nestles against the island but can move when needed.

▲ This ultramodern island marries industrial materials with avant-garde design. A steel sheet forms a breakfast bar, then folds down to shape a backsplash for the cooktop and work counter below. Steel brackets bolted together make up the legs and supports.

▶ Not all islands are rectangles, nor do they always dominate the kitchen. Here, a square island bridges the gap between counters of different heights and materials. Atop the table's alder base is a 12-inch-thick maple butcher block.

◄ Before | The existing L-shaped kitchen was small and dark, with high-contrast cabinetry. A tiny nursery on one side and a bedroom on the other offered options for expansion.

In keeping with the proportions of the room, the island is smaller than usual; the open grid base prevents it from looking bulky.

▶ **A pantry,** washer/dryer, water heater, and mini-office hide behind sliding doors, reducing visual clutter and supplying deep storage for large items. The grid on the lighting unit above the desk echoes the island's base.

◀ # After | Removing walls between the kitchen and adjoining rooms created nearly twice as much space. The freestanding island and frameless cabinets are maple; red oak strip flooring matches floors in the living and dining rooms.

New double-hung windows brighten the room and afford a wide view of the garden. Divided lights on the upper sashes are a nod to Craftsman and Bungalow design.

Components of stainless steel—range, backsplash, and countertop with integral sink—reflect the natural light and lend a seamless look to the room's surfaces.

▶ **The shallow storage and display unit** takes up most of the wall opposite the windows. Upper cabinets are 12 inches deep; those below, a more generous 18.

NOTES FROM THE ARCHITECT

"Storage walls are a good solution for small kitchens. They free up space and keep the kitchen from looking like a cabinet showroom."

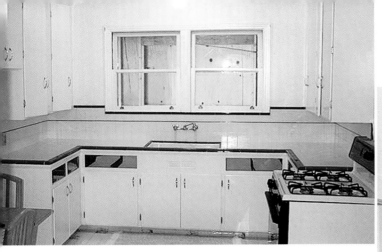

▲ Before | The original

kitchen was in fair condition, but it lacked a dishwasher, garbage disposer, and access to the backyard. Dated cabinets with chrome handles and dingy yellow tile with brown trim just had to go.

The homeowners | After ▶

thought they wanted a traditional white kitchen until a visit to a French kitchen store in Quebec reshaped their vision. They thoroughly researched their options, enlisted the help of a color consultant, and went from an all-white plan to a three-color palette of ivory, khaki, and red.

Kitchen continues ▶ ▶

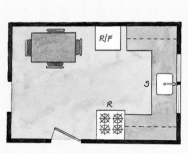

BEFORE

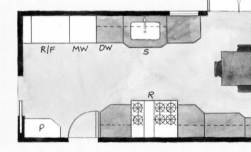

AFTER

Floor plans: An 8-foot addition at one end opened up the kitchen, allowing for a window seat and French doors. There's now room for twice the storage, plus display space.

100

◀ **To soften the lines** of the longish galley kitchen, the design called for "cutting corners" on the cabinets at either end of the room and varying the depths of perimeter cabinets and granite countertops.

▶ **An unmatched assortment** of pulls and knobs brings a fresh look to full-overlay doors and drawers.

▼ **A small desk** tucked between base cabinets provides a convenient station for light paperwork; slots above keep things organized.

▲ **Corner cabinets form "bookends"** for a built-in window seat faced with bead-board; its top lifts for additional storage. The cabinet shown here anchors the desk and affords a smooth visual transition to the adjacent wall.

Kitchen continues ▶ ▶

"You can order a range like ours with a 12-inch riser splash on the back, but that leaves a mostly blank wall above. Our contractor suggested we get a sheet of stainless steel, cut to fit, from a local metal shop. The contractor glued the sheet to the wall, and we now have an inexpensive backsplash that's good-looking and easy to clean."

◄ **The pantry** takes advantage of corner space, yet its angled footprint does not intrude into the traffic pattern. The red door to the garage echoes the accent wall; a glass pocket door leads to the dining room.

▼ **Custom cabinetry includes cubbies** for the homeowner's collection of painted-wood chickens. She might also stow long kitchenwares like rolling pins in the open boxes.

Color Palette

Knobs on the new range and fabric for the window seat inspired the earthy red of the accent wall and the door next to the pantry. Creamy ivory warms up the cabinets yet "reads" as a neutral; khaki walls show off cabinet detailing and link the other colors.

◄ **French doors with single panes** (rather than divided lights) bring welcome light into the kitchen and make for a charming patio entrance.

DESIGN TIP

To make your cabinets pop, paint them a different color (usually lighter) than the walls.

◄ Before | In spite of the knotty paneling, dark cabinets, and brown tile of the old kitchen and dining room, the new owners of this lakeside retreat sensed the potential for one open, organized space in which to cook and entertain.

With walls removed and the **After ▶** ceiling raised, the space acquired the "bones" needed for a light-filled kitchen outfitted in materials chosen for durable, rather than trendy, appeal. Two sinks, two refrigerators (one in a base cabinet), and two separate ovens ensure flexibility and convenience for an avid cook.

Oversized (18-inch) ceramic tiles, set "on point" for interest, make up the neutral backsplash.

◄ Reflecting the woodsy environs of the home, custom-made face-frame cabinets with partial-overlay doors and extra-deep crown molding show off the combined beauties of birch and red alder. A six-burner cooktop is well positioned near the smaller oven and prep sink; the stainless steel hood includes plate-warming racks.

Remote-control skylights with shades admit or block light year-round and, when open, are a welcome means of releasing fierce summer heat.

Angled display shelves facing outward help link the new dining area and expanded kitchen.

A tiered peninsula with granite countertop and breakfast bar provides another work station closer to a gathering spot for guests.

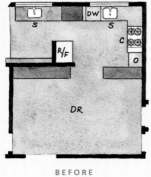

BEFORE

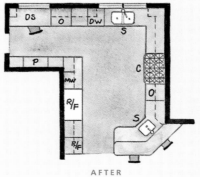

AFTER

Floor plans: The original kitchen consisted of a longish galley, interrupted by a short wall and the refrigerator. New plans called for an L-shaped layout, with part of the kitchen extending into the former dining room.

▼Before | Mismatched cabinets, outmoded appliances, and worn surfaces made for a kitchen that was neither attractive

nor efficient. A door to the basement (at left) precluded using the corner for storage.

"An eat-in | After▶ kitchen with lots of light"

topped the homeowners' wish list, and by every measure that dream was realized. White frameless cabinets with frame-and-panel doors combine traditional and contemporary design; supporting surfaces— a tile backsplash, granite countertops, and soothing green walls—complement the new kitchen's clean lines.

Kitchen continues ▶ ▶

Starting their all-over home remodel with the kitchen proved a wise move:
"The kitchen set the style for the rest of the house. In making decisions and choices for the kitchen,
we learned what we liked and wanted, and everything else just flowed."

◄ **Pendant light fixtures** with milky glass shades and a brushed-stainless finish provide task lighting. A bead-and-chain roller shade mounted inside the casing is a practical choice for an over-sink window.

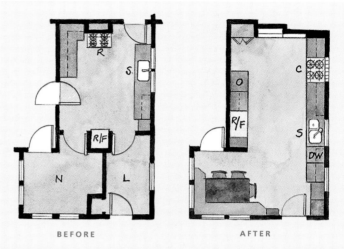

BEFORE   AFTER

Floor plans: Fragmented and dark, the back of the house included a breakfast nook with barely enough room for a table, a passageway laundry, and a kitchen with the refrigerator positioned between two doors. Eliminating an interior wall and relocating the laundry upstairs turned the jumble of rooms into the heart of the home.

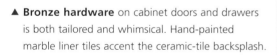

▲ **Bronze hardware** on cabinet doors and drawers is both tailored and whimsical. Hand-painted marble liner tiles accent the ceramic-tile backsplash.

◄ **A shallow spice niche,** base cabinets, and open bookshelves streamline a wall that previously included a protruding enclosure for ductwork and wiring as well as cabinets of varying depths. On the adjacent wall, a glass-block backsplash blurs an undesirable south-facing view while bathing the cooktop area in diffuse light.

▶ **Single-sash casement windows** with divided lights were chosen for their compatibility with existing double-hung, divided-light windows throughout the house. The pedestal table is narrower than usual, to fit the space.

‹Before | A dark, walled-in duplex kitchen offered little room to maneuver, for the cook or others. The designer/homeowner knew what to do: open the kitchen to the dining and living areas.

Undercabinet lights shine on a backsplash made up of 1-inch glass tile. Stainless steel windowsills echo other metal elements in the room.

A stainless steel sink increases the food prep possibilities on the island. The butcher-block counter serves as both a cutting and serving surface.

Integral-color plaster covers the walls and sides of the island in rich, rustic color. Seen up close, the surface reveals streaks or flecks of color from ground-up mineral oxides present in the plaster.

CAN.TOMATOS
CELERY
NANAS
APPLES
GRAPEJUICE
BERRIES
GOATMILK
TOFU
GARLIC-SHALLO
BEER
GOAT CHEESE

▼After | The essence of eclectic style, the combined kitchen and dining area is a rich blend of natural and man-made materials, in a space that is at once everyday and unique. Varied surfaces (wood, steel, tile, plaster) and cabinetry (solid front, glass front, open) keep the galley layout interesting.

▶ **A solid-core door,** cut to fit, teams up with an inexpensive pullout shelving unit to create the tandem pantry. Blackboard paint on both sides helps blend the pantry with the refrigerator.

The refrigerator and range doors, originally black, were powder-coated a dark gray for greater compatibility with the muted palette.

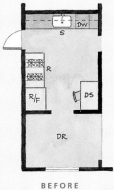

BEFORE

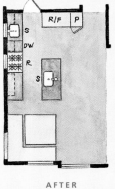

AFTER

Floor plans: With the interior walls gone, the kitchen feels like an integral part of the larger space. A built-in banquette takes up less room than a table and chairs; an island adds needed counter space.

111

▲ **Before** | This open-plan kitchen hardly qualified as a "problem room," but the space had long outgrown its country styling. The cabinets were still in good repair, but other surfaces and components were ready for replacement.

With no need to | **After** ▸ change the room's footprint, the makeover plan focused on replicating the rich hues and natural textures of Tuscany. Walls the summery color of straw look and feel like real fresco; granite tiles offer the elegance and durability of real stone, with a lower cost than slab granite.

Kitchen continues ▸ ▸

◄ **Turned legs on the island** give it the look of freestanding furniture. Crumpled pieces of brown paper bags pasted to the sides, then rubbed with wax, create a surface that resembles worn leather.

▶ **Replacement "skins"** update the existing dishwasher. A sheet-metal supplier can cut 24-gauge brushed–stainless steel pieces to size. The switch is easy to do: the skins slide out or in when the side screws are loosened.

▼ **Resin trim pieces** finished to look like metal contribute another Tuscan touch to the scheme.

▲ **Granite tile** covers the countertops, island, and backsplash. To de-emphasize the tile joints, the grout color closely matches the tones of the granite.

◄ **Faux fresco** adds mottled color and varied texture to plain walls. The substance is simply a mixture of joint compound and universal paint tint, applied with a metal drywall-taping knife.

With no plans **Before** ▶ to enlarge the original kitchen— nor space to create a walk-in pantry—maximizing storage in the existing space was the top priority. Countertops were in good shape but decades old.

The relief ceramic-tile backsplash introduces texture and mottled color to the scheme and serves as an understated focal point.

Frameless maple cabinets **After** ▶ with full-overlay doors and raised panels set a warm, traditional tone while providing plenty of storage in the new space. A granite breakfast bar straddles the imaginary line between the kitchen and eating area, linking the two rooms.

◀ **Upper-cabinet doors and drawers** flanking the refrigerator are set back 3 inches to avoid the visual weight of a solid wall of cabinetry. Faux columns at the corners add decorative detailing to the base cabinets.

Floor plans: The appliances remain on the same walls in the new plan, with the exception of the microwave. Granite countertops with angled corners and upper cabinets set on the diagonal soften the lines.

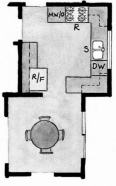

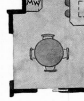

BEFORE

AFTER

A cabinetry hood installed over a metal liner is a simple solution for a small-space range.

A matching wood valance with decorative appliqués dresses up the over-sink window.

Brushed-pewter and white ceramic pulls and knobs make fitting hardware for cabinets with a white glaze finish.

▲ Before | Entertaining

was out of the question in the space of the original kitchen— little more than 100 square feet. And for the wife, who cooks, and the husband, who cleans up, it was an entirely inadequate work space.

Clean, crisp, and | **After ▶**

classic, the all-white space is a calm respite from hectic city living and a dream kitchen for the homeowners. A large island topped with marble anchors the layout; frameless cabinets maximize interior storage. The curved stainless steel range hood includes a utensil shelf and banded trim.

A stainless steel bread drawer, a sleek version of an old-fashioned kitchen accoutrement, occupies a base cabinet next to the range. Look for bread-drawer kits online and in storage specialty shops.

▶ **Gentle light floods the new family room** through large windows, skylights, and a central clerestory. The peninsula resembles a piece of furniture more than a kitchen cabinet—its beechwood surface has a table's edging, and its base differs in frame style and detailing. A river rock–faced fireplace and limestone-topped hearth make subtle reference to the kitchen's marble countertops.

▼ **An integral "drainboard"** cut into the marble streamlines the cleanup zone. Statuary-vein marble, a subcategory of Carrara marble, has both pronounced and subtle veining, from near black to faint gray.

▲ **Open shelving** is in keeping with the simplicity of an all-white kitchen. These wide shelves span the wall and hold tableware that the homeowners use daily.

▶ **Adjustable metal shelves** maximize storage in a blind-corner cabinet. When you pull out the door, it swivels to the side to reveal attached baskets; interior baskets slide forward within reach. As the door is closed, both components glide back into place.

120

Kitchen continues ▶ ▶

BEFORE

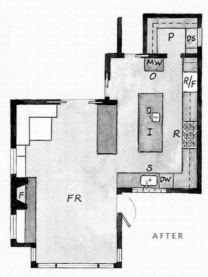

AFTER

Floor plans: Appropriating an existing deck plus an additional 8 feet and then reconfiguring the kitchen and family room resulted in the expansive, free-flowing space the homeowners longed for. The peninsula forms a natural boundary between the two areas.

◀ **A walk-in pantry** doubles as command central: at its small desk the homeowner plans menus, makes phone calls, and takes care of household business. Open shelves and baskets hold an assortment of kitchenwares and nonperishables.

▶ **The upper cabinet boxes** included doors in early plans, but the cook opted for open storage instead: "If I can see it, I know I'll use it." Flip-out doors reveal a stand-alone microwave and a small TV, with an adjustable shelf between them to allow for changes down the road.

▲ **A compost bin** in the island counter collects produce scraps. The opening was cut prior to the countertop's installation; the cabinetmaker designed a drawer underneath just deep enough to hold the bin.

▶ **Retractable flip-out doors** open like regular doors; when they are at right angles to the cabinet, they slide back into the base. Three shallow pullout shelves accommodate baking accessories.

LESSONS FROM THE HOMEOWNERS

As they packed in preparation for the remodel, the homeowners inventoried their wares, planning on paper where everything would go in the new cupboards and drawers. "If you're a perfectionist about where you will store things and how the space will function," one of them said, "you can relax and work with your new kitchen, because it will be working with you."

A Storage Sampler

"We need more storage!" is a common cry of homeowners in pursuit of the perfect kitchen. And for good reason: the better organized the kitchen, the more efficiently it functions.

Happily, manufacturers have obliged homeowners with an abundance of storage options. Whether you have the luxury of specifying custom-made cabinets—and their highly detailed interiors—or you're adding ready-made inserts to existing cabinetry, you'll find products to please. And if you're looking for a unique solution to storage, one that adds to the character of your kitchen, consider freestanding furniture pieces.

◄ A riser or tiered rack won't add shelf space, but it greatly enhances the visibility of the cabinet's contents.

▲ Oils, spices, and condiments are never more than a glide away in drawers with slanted and upright organizer inserts.

▶ This marble-topped buffet only looks old; in fact, it was designed to blend with—yet distinguish itself from—contemporary, built-in cabinetry in a small kitchen (see pages 40–41). Appliances are stowed behind the doors; jars on shelves above hold grains, pasta, and nuts.

▼ On a swivel platform attached to the door of a custom cabinet, the TV can be seen by the cook and by those seated at the banquette, then disappears at homework time (see pages 106–109).

▲ A "mudroom" entrance to this kitchen (see pages 62–63) contains smart built-in storage for everyone in the family. The upper cabinets, file drawers, and open shelves hold kitchen-related items and household papers; lower cubbies, a bench, and coat hooks are mostly for the kids and their gear.

▶ A freestanding cabinet, custommade to fit the microwave, frees up counter space and fits the style of an older home. Side towel bars and a wine rack attached to the lower shelf were constructed from copper tubing and wire.

▶ Recyclables stay organized and out of sight in bins mounted on a pullout base cabinet.

◄ Before
A ho-hum galley kitchen in this 1960s ranch-style house needed a boost—on a budget. The newish appliances could stay, and the original cabinets needed only a facelift.

Cross-reeded glass in new cabinet doors adds a bit of sparkle to the square-pattern scheme. A cabinetmaker can measure, order, and install new doors for existing cabinets.

Commercial-grade vinyl tile squares are not hard to install, provided that you prep the subflooring and spread a leveling compound before applying the tile adhesive.

▶ **An 11-inch-deep pantry** was custom made to hide the side of the refrigerator and augment existing storage.

The colorful valance, reminiscent of 1950s oilcloth, consists of fabric squares stitched between two sheets of clear craft vinyl.

◀ **After** | The homeowner's Amish-style quilt was the color and pattern catalyst for this blah-to-bright retro makeover. The checkerboard floor, a signature feature of mid-20th-century kitchens, makes the strongest design statement; grasshopper green walls link multicolored accents.

◀ **Plain and prefabricated-mosaic glass tiles** on the backsplash evoke the quilt's large and small colored squares. Because glass tile is thinner than standard ceramic tile, it requires a special (but inexpensive) underlayment.

127

▼**Before** | Open yet oppressive, the kitchen, dining room, and living room in this 1970s house were dark; the lack of crossing light exacerbated the cavelike atmosphere.

"From its | **After** ▶ inception," says the architect, "this design was all about light." A glass-block window and a skylight bathe the galley in soft, even light; pendant fixtures help suggest the separation between island and dining area within the flowing space. A metal railing similarly establishes the living room's boundary.

Kitchen continues ▶ ▶

128

◄ **The 12-inch-high island backsplash** conceals the food prep and cleanup zone from seated dinner guests. This detail enables the kitchen to seem organized even when it's not.

► **Maple-veneer plywood cabinets** and highly figured granite countertops introduce natural patterns into the geometric scheme.

▲ **A low-profile recessed hood,** installed on the underside of the upper cabinets, sets the color vocabulary for black accents throughout the room. When the hood slides out and clicks into place, the fan goes on.

◄ **Elongated Japanese hardware** with a brushed-metal finish contributes to the austere aesthetic.

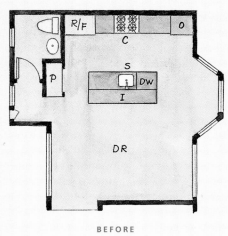

BEFORE

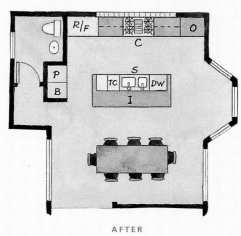

AFTER

Floor plans: The similarities in the old and new layouts belie the dramatic changes wrought by new surfaces and components. The cooktop and sink remain in their original positions, to take best advantage of light from new sources.

Before | The 8-by-17-foot kitchen was barely large enough for the cook, let alone a family of five. More space was the first priority; next was achieving a traditional look while using modern appliances and contemporary color.

This light-filled space—with two | **After** ▶ work zones, two ovens (handy for a home with three kids), a spacious dining area, and lots of storage—is everyone's favorite place in the home. Say the homeowners, who are both architects, "It's the perfect spot to start and end the day."

Most cabinets are undercounter style, to maximize windows and keep supplies at a child's height.

◀ **A handsomely proportioned built-in hutch** resembles furniture and melds the kitchen with the dining area. The oak dining table is lit by 1950s-inspired glass pendant lights.

A clean and contemporary stainless steel hood also serves as a display and storage shelf. Its underside is packed with task lighting.

Reminiscent of old-fashioned pie safes, cabinets with flip-up, perforated-panel doors hold a variety of small appliances and cookbooks.

The renovation made way for a 4-by-7-foot island topped with granite and equipped with a prep sink, convection oven, and breakfast bar.

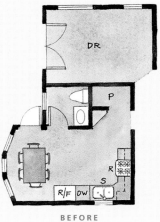

BEFORE

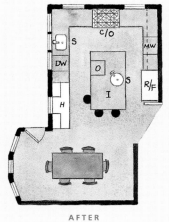

AFTER

Floor plans: In removing the wall between the kitchen and dining room, the homeowners eliminated a walk-in pantry and relocated a powder room. The kitchen and dining areas change places in the new plan, allowing more room for appliances and cabinetry.

133

▲ Before | Although

the existing kitchen was hardly
a disaster, its floor plan wasted
space and ignored potential
storage. Two ranges, side by
side, were one more than
needed.

A mix of natural | After ▶

materials and components
conveys the old-world style
and ambience that the homeowners desired. Stained and
distressed alder wood cabinets have flush-inset doors
and drawers, handblown glass
in their upper doors, and
fanciful metal pulls. Granite
counters and red oak flooring
are both colorful and rustic.

▼ **Open storage** punctuates a long run of base cabinets. The woven baskets slide in and out on wood runners, also known as glides.

▲ **Hand-painted 6-inch-square marble tiles** blend beautifully with the colors and patterns of the counters and backsplash; marble trim pieces cap the splash.

▶ **The custom range hood** began as a standard metal liner; it was then covered with a wood frame and layers of plaster, sealed to preserve the natural color. Tumbled marble and ceramic tiles in intricate Celtic patterns make up the backsplash.

◀ **Tucked under the lower end of the stairs,** cabinets and open shelving convert an awkward space into a pantry.

▲ **The stacked washer and dryer,** located under the high end of the stairs, stay hidden behind tall cabinet doors.

◀ **The old-world theme continues** in the deep, farmhouse-style sink and pump-handle faucet. Costa Esmeralda granite on the counters and windowsill is streaked with dark green, white, and gold veining.

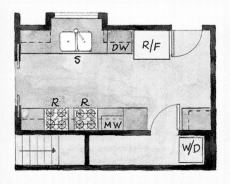

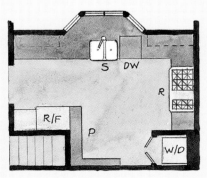

Floor plans: Eliminating the back door allowed for a focal-point placement of the professional-style range. With the interior wall removed, there's easy access to the new pantry.

BEFORE

AFTER

137

◄Before As part of a whole-house remodel, the small kitchen in this 1950s rancher was in line for a makeover. It began by pushing out the sink wall toward the backyard.

Pendant lights are fitted with powder-coated gray metal shades; white enamel on the inside bounces the light.

Sparkling stainless steel is a recurring design element. On the sinks, faucets, shelving, and the main countertops it is sleek and practical; the range with matching hood is a focal point as well.

The solid-surface island countertop has the look of concrete but the stain resistance and easy care of resin-and-mineral composite materials.

▼ After

Clean, modern, and functional, the new space is the result of the architect's flexible design as well as the homeowners' dogged pursuit of just-right appliances, fixtures, and surfaces.

Their efforts paid off: "Hardly a day goes by that we don't think about how happy we are with the outcome."

▼ **Silvery moss green** laminate cabinets with high-style handles reflect the homeowners' contemporary aesthetic. In the background is a wall of teal laminate cabinets, including a matching-panel refrigerator. Underfoot, 12-inch composite tiles with bits of natural stone suspended in resin are resilient and durable.

▼ **A spacious island** does double duty as breakfast bar and food prep zone. On the far side of the room, pocket doors flanking the range can close off the kitchen from the dining room.

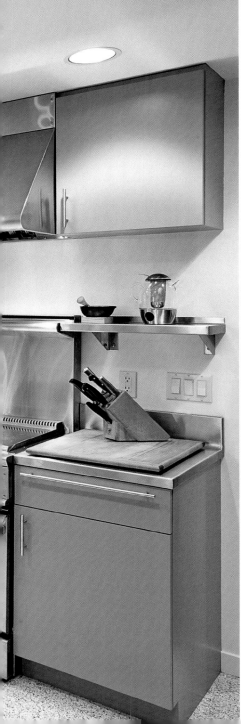

With three doorways— **Before** ▶
one of them leading outside—the tiny
kitchen was more thoroughfare than room.
The homeowner hoped to bring the ambience of the garden inside; enlarging the
space and maximizing storage were two
more practical goals.

Open yet cozy, the new **After** ▶
kitchen achieves the indoor/outdoor
connection that inspired the remodel,
while delivering a work core that's
convenient and efficient. Granite
countertops and strip oak flooring are
warm and natural.

◀ **Tall casement windows** with fixed glass above offer
sweeping views of the hillside garden. A breakfront on
the interior wall provides extra storage; upper cabinets
are 12 inches deep, lower ones 18.

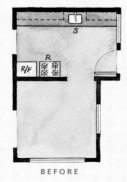

BEFORE

AFTER

Floor plans: Eliminating the short wall between
the kitchen and dining room and bumping out the
latter in both directions turned the two spaces
into a single larger one. To free up the sink wall
for windows, the architect located a pantry and
broom closet on the facing wall, behind cabinets,
and moved the exterior door to the dining room.

The backsplash becomes a focal point at the end of the short galley. The central panel is 1-inch marble mosaic and 2-inch corner glass tile; the surrounding tile is Jerusalem limestone.

Using different counter surfaces appealed to the homeowner, who wanted something softer than granite atop this short run of cabinets. Butcher block fit the bill and introduced another material from nature.

Facing the dishwasher with a matching panel makes the appliance all but disappear and maintains the visual flow of the base cabinetry.

Design and Photography Credits

Index